What's Living in Your Classroom?

Andrew Solway

Heinemann Library
Chicago, Illinois

Customer Service 888-454-2279
Visit our website at www.heinemannlibrary.com

Designed by David Poole and Paul Myerscough
Illustrations by Geoff Ward
Originated by Dot Gradations
Printed and bound in China by South China Printing Company

08 07 06 05 04
10 9 8 7 6 5 4 3 2 1

Library of Congress Cataloging-in-Publication Data
Solway, Andrew.
  What's living in your classroom? / Andrew Solway.
      v. cm. -- (Hidden life)
Includes bibliographical references and index.
Contents: Under the microscope -- Microbes in the muck -- Feeling lousy
-- Micro-plants -- Ear mites -- Billions of bacteria -- Microbe-packed
food -- Chocolate microbes? -- Colds and flu -- Allergy alert -- Chewing
up old books.
  ISBN 1-4034-4846-9 (HC library binding) -- ISBN 1-4034-5485-X (PB)
  1. Microbiology--Juvenile literature. 2. Insects--Juvenile
literature. [1. Microorganisms.] I. Title. II. Series.
  QR57.S65 2004
  579'.1755--dc22
                              2003018004

Acknowledgments
The author and publishers are grateful to the following for permission to reproduce copyright
material: p 4a Getty images/photodisk; p. 4b Science Photo Library (Dr Tony Brain and David
Parker), p. 5 (Philippe Plailly Eurolios), pp. 6a, 25 (Dr Jeremy Burgess), p. 6b (Andrew Syred),
pp. 7, 17a (Rosenfeld Images Ltd), p. 9 (Sinclair Stammers), p. 10b (M I Walker),
p. 11 (Jan Hinsch), pp. 13, 22a (Eye of Science), pp. 15a, 16 (David Scharf), p. 15b (Andrew
Syred), p. 20 (Linda Steinmark, Custom Medical Stock Photo), pp. 21a, 23 (A B Dowsett),
p. 21b (Dr Linda Stannard, UCT), p. 22b (Damien Lovegrove); pp. 8a, 8b Science Photo
Library; p. 10a Alamy; p. 12 NHPA (Michael Leach); p. 14 Martin Sookias; p. 17b Corbis
(Jacqui Hurst), p. 18a (Charles Gupton), p. 18b (George D Lepp); p. 19 Medical-on-line; p. 24
Ardea (Steve Hopkins); p. 26 Oxford Scientific Films (Tony Bomford), p. 27 (Harold Taylor).

Cover photograph of a head louse, reproduced with permission of Science Photo Library.

Our thanks to Dr. Philip Parrillo, entomologist at the Field Museum in Chicago, for his
comments in the preparation of this book.

Every effort has been made to contact copyright holders of any material reproduced in this
book. Any omissions will be rectified in subsequent printings if notice is given to the
publishers.

Some words are shown in bold, **like this.** You can find out
what they mean by looking in the glossary.

Contents

Many of the photos in this book were taken using a microscope.
In the captions you may see a number that tells you how much
they have been enlarged. For example, a photo marked
"(x200)" is about 200 times bigger than in real life.

Under the Microscope

During the school day, a classroom is full of life. But at night and on weekends, there is not much life—is there? Well, you may have plants in your classroom, or a fish tank or pets, but even if you don't, there is plenty of life around the classroom. You just have to look closely enough.

If you could look at your classroom through a microscope, you would see all kinds of living things that are completely invisible to the naked eye— a world of hidden life.

This photo (x200) shows clumps of bacteria on the point of a pin (at this magnification the point looks flat). It gives some idea of just how tiny bacteria are.

This classroom looks empty, but you can find hidden life everywhere if you look hard enough.

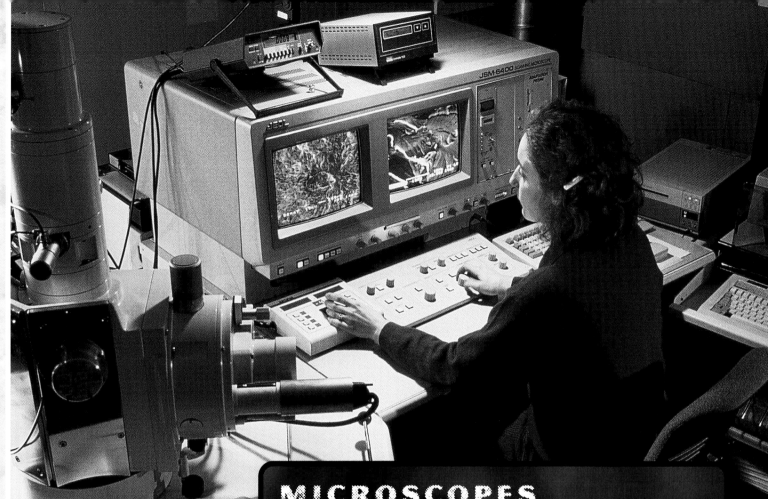

Getting up close

Even at low magnification, you can find creatures with your microscope. For instance, you might find that a small stain in a damp corner of the room is made up of a mass of tiny threads. It is a **mold fungus,** a relative of mushrooms.

Moving closer

If you zoom in closer, you will start to see microscopic creatures everywhere. The most common of them are

MICROSCOPES

We know what tiny creatures such as bacteria and viruses look like because scientists have been able to use microscopes to study them. A light microscope— the type of microscope you may have used yourself at home or at school—can magnify objects up to about 1,800 times. But to look at really tiny things, scientists use **electron microscopes.** This kind of microscope can magnify objects up to 500,000 times.

bacteria. These simple-looking creatures are made up of just a single **cell.** An average-sized bacterium is around a few micrometers (millionths of a meter) long.

Smallest of all

If you increase the magnification of your

microscope to its limit, you might be able to see the smallest creatures of all— **viruses.** Viruses cannot survive without the help of a living cell. They reproduce by getting inside a cell and taking it over. They then use the cell to produce thousands more viruses.

Microbes in Muck

You probably have a coatroom at school where you can leave your coat and shoes. This is good because otherwise you might bring in all sorts of unwelcome visitors!

*Bits of soil, shown in green on the right, are home to all kinds of **bacteria** and other microbes. Dung microbes are sometimes found in soil and can include the bacteria Escherichia coli (sometimes called E. coli) and **fungi** such as Pilobolus (shown below).*

The soles of your shoes have bits of dirt and mud stuck to them. When you arrive at school, you bring this dirt with you. If you live on a farm or in the country, this dirt could include interesting things like animal dung.

Microbes in mud and dung

Yuck! Mud and dung sound like horrible places for any creature to live. But for **microbes,** mud and dung—especially dung—are rich sources of food.

All kinds of microbes live in dung. They make up almost a third of its weight. The rest of the living world relies on these microbes because they break down the dung into nutrients that enrich the soil. Without these microbes, we would be surrounded everywhere by piles of dung.

Treating sewage

Because bacteria are so good at digesting dung, we use them to treat **sewage** (the human waste from our

towns and cities). Sewage is packed with dung microbes. At a sewage treatment plant, waste is mixed with water and pumped into large tanks. Air is then bubbled through the water to help the microbes in it to grow. The microbes change the sewage into **carbon dioxide** and other harmless chemicals.

Making you sick

Although dung microbes are useful, it is important that they do not get into the wrong places because they can make people ill. For instance if *E. coli* bacteria get onto food, they can cause food poisoning.

🔘 *In a sewage treatment plant, sewage is digested by microbes in tanks like these.*

BACTERIA FACTS

You could fit about 1,000 average-sized bacteria across a pinhead. They may be round, rod-shaped, comma-shaped, or spiral. Most bacteria have a hard outer wall and sometimes a layer of sticky slime outside that.

Bacteria can use all kinds of materials as food. Some bacteria actually eat rubber, and others even eat gasoline.

feeling Lousy

If you have an itchy head, you might have tiny guests in your hair. Head lice are small, flattened insects that hide in people's hair and feed on their blood. Anyone can get head lice, especially in a busy, crowded classroom.

Parasitic passengers

Head lice are **parasites**—they live on humans (their hosts) and get all their nourishment from human blood. Lice cannot fly or jump. They move from **host** to host by simply walking from one person's head to another.

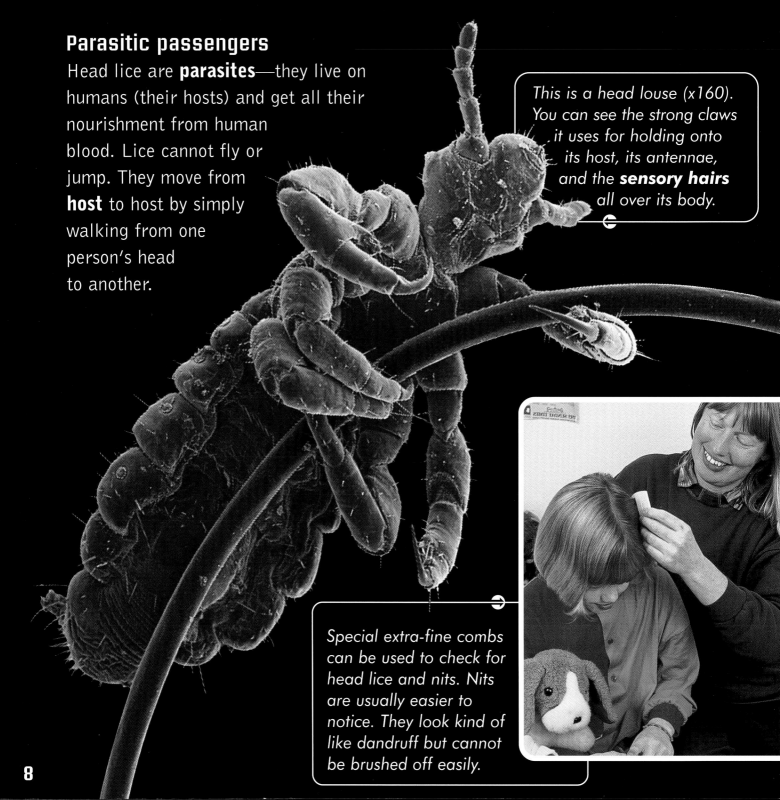

*This is a head louse (x160). You can see the strong claws it uses for holding onto its host, its antennae, and the **sensory hairs** all over its body.*

Special extra-fine combs can be used to check for head lice and nits. Nits are usually easier to notice. They look kind of like dandruff but cannot be brushed off easily.

In a busy, crowded place like a school this can easily happen, so once lice get into one person's hair, they often get spread around.

Hard to spot

Head lice are well-suited to their parasitic lifestyle. They are tiny—little bigger than a pinhead—and dull brown in color, which makes them hard to spot in hair. Their bodies are flattened and they have strong claws for holding onto hairs.

Lice have no eyes because in the thick forest of a person's hair, sight is not very useful. They rely instead on their senses of smell and touch to find their way around. They eat by biting a tiny hole in the scalp and sucking out blood.

Head lice take only about three weeks to grow from eggs to adults, so their numbers can increase very quickly. However, they live for only about 30 days.

Female lice stick their egg cases, called nits, to hairs, very close to the scalp. When they hatch, the young lice look like small adults. They take about a week to grow to full size.

Getting rid of lice

Normal shampoo or combing cannot get rid of lice. You need a special shampoo to get rid of adult lice. Nits are harder to get rid of. Regular combing with an extra-fine nit comb is the best way to remove them.

Below is a louse nit with a developing louse inside. At this stage the egg case is almost see-through, which makes it very hard to see.

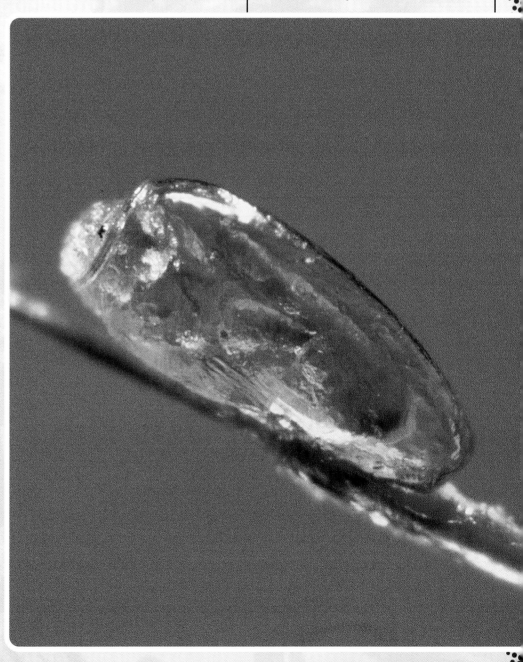

Micro-Plants

Some classrooms have an aquarium. It's fun to watch the fish, and they are easy to take care of. But sometimes the water gets all green and scummy, or a green film forms on the glass. These problems are caused by microscopic plantlike creatures called **algae.**

Fish are not the only living things in an aquarium.

Most algae such as Spirogyra reproduce by simply dividing in two. But sometimes two filaments will join up, as here. Once this has happened, the algae form thick-walled **spores,** which can survive cold and drying out.

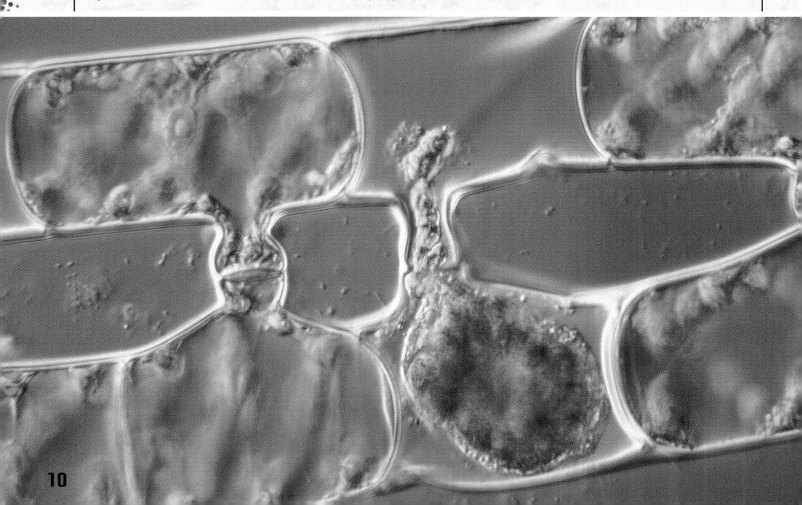

Sun worshippers

Like plants, green algae need sunlight to survive. This is because they do not eat food, but make it from water, sunlight, and **carbon dioxide.**

Plants and algae are green because they contain a colored chemical called **chlorophyll.** Chlorophyll is a key part of the process for making food using sunlight energy. Just like plant **cells,** algae have **chloroplasts,** which contain chlorophyll. In chloroplasts sunlight energy is turned into sugary food.

Spirals and star filaments

Green algae are microscopic, but some of them join together to make long strings, or filaments. One of the best known of these algae is *Spirogyra.* They get their name from the fact that they have a long, spiral chloroplast. A related group of algae, called *Zygnema,* have star-shaped chloroplasts.

Skeletons of glass

Not all green algae are green. Some are brown! The brown stains that sometimes form on the glass of an aquarium are caused by algae called **diatoms.** Diatoms contain chlorophyll, but they also have other pigments that make them look brown.

Under the microscope, diatoms are tiny jewels. Each kind of diatom has its own particular, beautifully shaped, glassy outer shell. The shell surface is covered in tiny fine lines. These lines are rows of tiny holes, which allow the cell inside to keep in touch with the outside world.

Freshwater diatoms (x240) come in a variety of shapes and sizes.

Ear Mites

Many classes have pet mice to take care of instead of fish. Mice can have problems with **parasites** called ear mites. Ear mites are smaller than head lice, but they are nastier. Luckily, they do not live on humans.

Mites are not insects, but close relatives of spiders, so they have eight legs rather than six. Ear mites can affect mice, dogs, cats, rabbits, and other pets, and a related kind of mite causes the skin disease *mange* in pets and some wild animals.

The irritation that ear mites cause makes the host animal, in this case a mouse, scratch itself and tear the skin.

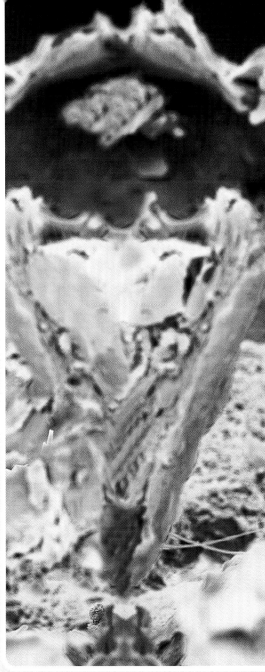

"Mitey" lives

Ear mites are hard to see, but microscopes show they have short legs and round bodies. When ear mites hatch, the **larvae** have only six legs. They feed on earwax and skin oils in the **host's** ear canal. After a week the larvae **molt** and become **protonymphs.** They then feed for three to five

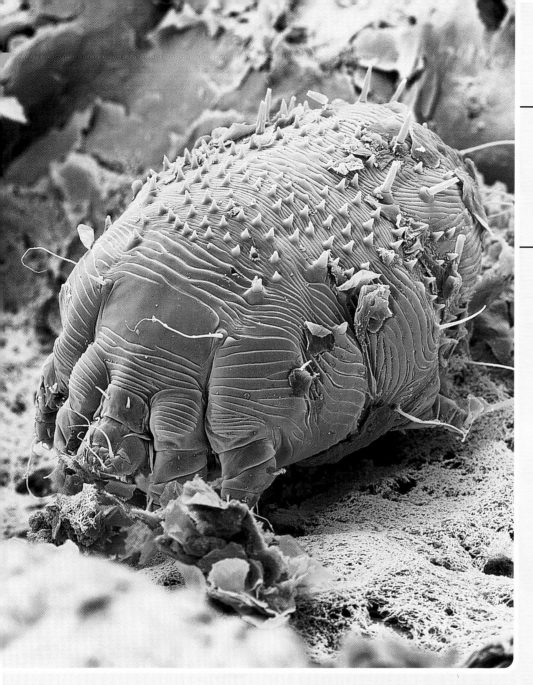

This photo shows an itch mite on the skin surface. Female itch mites are about 0.02 inch (0.5 mm) long, while males are smaller.

Ill effects

When ear mites first get into an animal, the host does not feel uncomfortable. But as mite numbers rise, their droppings and the poisons they produce make the ears sore and itchy, and they produce too much wax. Scratching causes the ears to bleed. Under a microscope, the dried blood from infected ears is crawling with mites.

days and molt again to become **deutonymphs.** Deutonymphs are strange creatures. Although they are not yet adults, they mate with male mites. Even more strange is that it is not clear at this stage what sex they will be as adults. After mating, deutonymphs molt again and become either male or female adults.

A "MITEY" BIG NUISANCE!

Mites and their larger relatives, ticks, cause all kinds of problems for people. Ticks and some mites are **parasites** on people or farm animals and pets. Other mites are plant pests, damaging food crops. But mites are not all bad. Mites that live in the soil help keep the soil fertile, and some **predatory** mites eat plant pests.

Billions of Bacteria

One of the main sources of hidden life in the classroom is you and your classmates. All of us carry **bacteria** around with us on our skin. Each person has about 1,000 billion skin bacteria—that's more than 160 times more bacteria than there are people in the world!

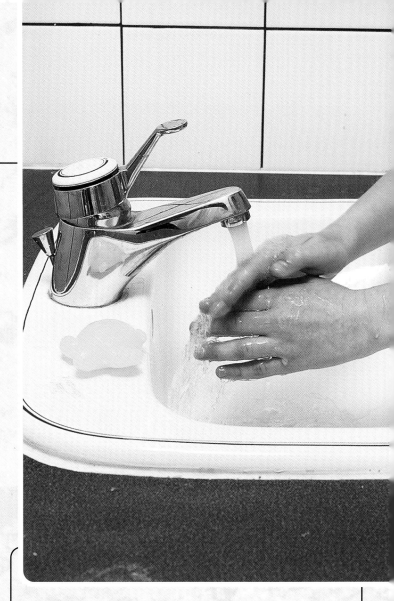

Skin bacteria prefer moist, warm places, and they need a source of food, usually sweat or skin oils. So there are more bacteria in warm, damp places, like the armpits, than on other parts of the skin.

Even though there can be many bacteria around the sink, washing your hands regularly is one of the best ways to avoid harmful germs.

Helpful bacteria

Skin bacteria do not usually do us any harm—in fact they help protect us from disease-causing bacteria. This is because it is hard for disease bacteria to survive and grow on the skin in competition with the bacteria that already live there.

Although your normal bacteria are not harmful, you do pick up foreign bacteria from other people and from things you touch. Some of these can cause disease, particularly if they get into your mouth or if you have a cut. This is why it is important to wash your hands before eating and to clean cuts.

Washing your hands

The areas around a sink are usually damp, and towels get damp regularly. Bacteria can grow in these areas, especially if towels are not changed regularly. Bacteria can even live on bars of soap if they are used very often and if they stay wet.

Despite this, washing your hands thoroughly with ordinary soap will get rid of nearly all the germs on them—even if the soap does have bacteria on it. But it is important to dry your hands well because bacteria can survive much better on wet hands.

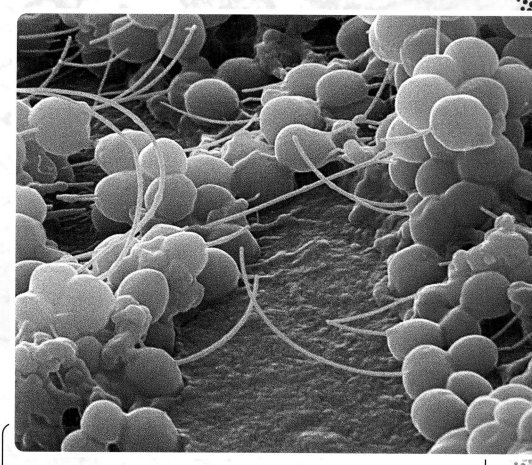

The bacteria Staphylococcus epidermidis (x17,700) are commonly found on human skin.

Below is a close-up of skin, showing dead **cells** flaking away from the surface.

BACTERIAL DEFENSES

The outer part of the skin is made up of about 15 layers of dead cells, cemented together with fats and oils. This is a tough barrier for bacteria to break through. Flakes of our skin are always being worn away, but they are replaced by new skin cells.

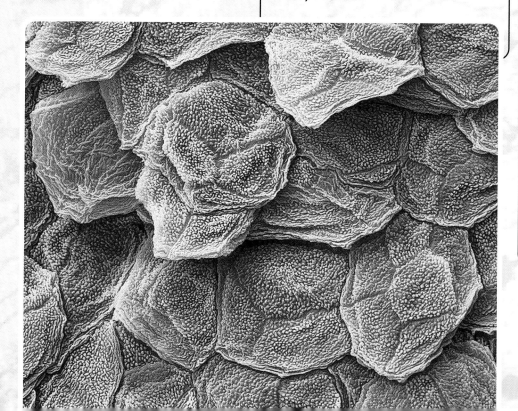

Microbe-Packed Food

Do you take a packed lunch to school? If you do, it might include a cheese sandwich and a yogurt. Both of these foods are full of **microbes.**

For thousands of years people have been making bread, yogurt, and cheese. All of these foods are made using microbes.

Bread

Without the help of microbes, bread would be flat and hard. To make it light and airy, you need to add yeast. Yeast is a microscopic creature—not a bacterium, but a type of **fungus.** The yeast feeds on the sugars in bread dough and produces **carbon dioxide** as a waste product. The carbon dioxide gets caught as tiny bubbles within the dough. These bubbles of carbon dioxide are what make the bread rise.

*Unlike other types of fungi, yeasts are single **cells** (x400), rather than tiny threads.*

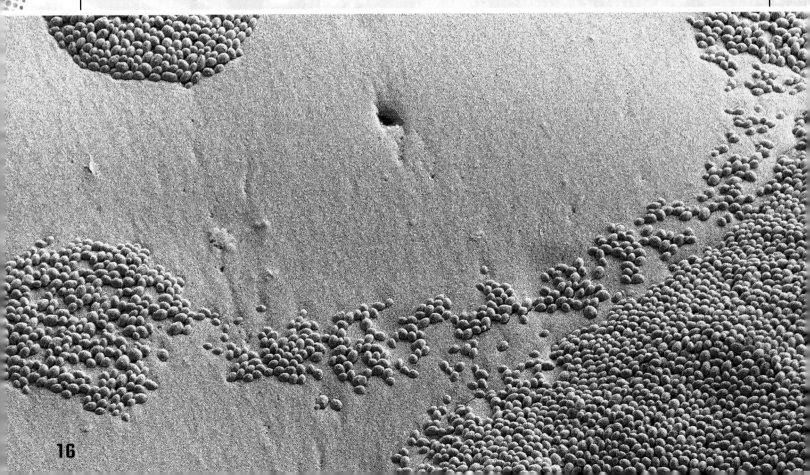

These raw cheeses depend on bacteria in order to ripen.

Cheese

Cheese is similar to yogurt in that it is made from milk and acid-producing bacteria. But cheese makers add another ingredient—**rennet**—which, along with the acid, makes the milk separate into milk solids called curds and a watery liquid called whey. The whey is drained off, then the curds are pressed—lightly at first, then with a pressure of several tons. The cheese is now left for a few months to ripen in a cool place. During this time bacteria continue to grow slowly and make further changes to the cheese, which improve its flavor.

*Some cheeses contain **fungi** as well as bacteria! The streaks in blue cheeses are produced by a **mold** fungus.*

Yogurt

Baking kills yeast, so when you eat bread, the microbes are already dead. But when you eat yogurt, the microbes are still alive, if it is live yogurt.

Yogurt is milk that is full of a special kind of **bacterium** called *Lactobacillus.* Like the yeast in bread, the *Lactobacillus* feeds on sugars in the milk. But unlike the yeast, it produces acid as a waste product. This acid is what gives the yogurt its sharp taste.

CHEESE FACTS

One gallon (4 liters) of milk (about 6.6 pounds, or 3 kg) yields less than a pound (0.5 kg) of cheese. The weight that is lost is all the water in milk.

Chocolate Microbes?

Maybe you have chocolate or candy with your packed lunch. There are no **microbes** in these foods, but microbes were needed for making them.

Making chocolate

Chocolate is made from cacao beans—the seeds of the cacao tree. The beans grow in a large pod. To make chocolate, workers pick the ripe pods, split them, and take out the beans. Then they pile up the beans, cover them with banana leaves, and leave them to **ferment.** Then they are dried and roasted.

Microbes have probably been used to make the food you eat for lunch.

Below is a ripe cacao pod split open to show the beans within.

The fermenting process takes away some of the bitterness of the cacao beans and develops their rich chocolatey flavor. Without this process, chocolate just wouldn't taste the same.

Fermentation relies on natural **bacteria** and yeasts, which feed on sugars in the beans. Air has to be kept out for fermentation to take place, which is why the beans are piled together and covered.

Gummy candies

Gummy bears and jelly candies contain a sweet, gummy substance called **xanthan** (pronounced zan-than). Xanthan is made by *Xanthomonas campestris* bacteria, and is used to thicken water into a gel. Besides sweets it is

Xanthomonas campestris bacteria themselves are yellow, but the xanthan gum they produce is colorless.

used to make ice cream, salad dressings, and some paints. *Xanthomonas* makes this gummy slime to keep itself from drying out.

AMAZING HONEY

Candies are full of sugar, so they should be good places for microbes to grow. But in fact microbes do not grow well in sugar. Honey is one substance that microbes really cannot live in. If it is kept in a sealed container, it will last for years without spoiling.

Colds and Flu

If you go to school with a cold, be careful to use a tissue if you cough or sneeze. Otherwise, you will spread a cloud of germs around the classroom. The germs that cause colds and flu are not bacteria. They are even smaller things called **viruses.**

The viruses that cause colds and flu spread from person to person on tiny droplets of liquid. These droplets fly into the air when an infected person coughs or sneezes. When someone else breathes in some of these droplets, they become infected. Luckily the body's defenses can usually fight off the infection, and we soon get better.

How do viruses work?

Viruses are unbelievably tiny packages of chemicals. They cannot grow or reproduce unless they can get inside the **cells** of another living thing. Viruses are very simple structures. The outside is a protective **protein** coat. Inside are the **genes** of the virus—the complex chemicals that make it possible for the virus to reproduce.

This photograph has caught the cloud of droplets that shoot out of the nose and mouth when a person sneezes. If the person has a cold or flu, many of these droplets will be carrying viruses.

When a virus gets into a cell, the virus's genes join themselves to the cell's genes. The virus's genes contain instructions that allow the virus to take over the cell's normal instructions. As a result, the cell becomes a virus-making factory, producing many copies.

Thousands of copies of the virus are made, and after a time the cell bursts, releasing the viruses to infect other cells.

Other viruses

Viruses cause many other diseases besides colds and flu. Mumps, sore throats, and the brain disease called *meningitis* are just some of the other diseases they cause in humans. And viruses infect just about all other types of living things, too—even **bacteria.**

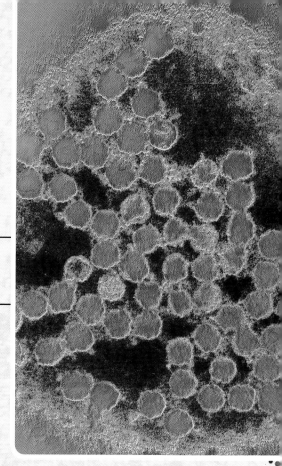

This photo shows a cluster of cold viruses (about x200,000).

NO METABOLISM

A living cell is like a chemical factory. One set of chemicals (the cell's food) is broken down to produce energy. This energy is then used to make other chemicals—the proteins and other substances that make up the cell. All of this chemical activity together is called the cell's **metabolism.**

Viruses have no metabolism. Instead, they take over the metabolism of a living cell.

These green blobs are influenza viruses (viruses that cause flu). They are seven or eight times bigger than the cold viruses shown above.

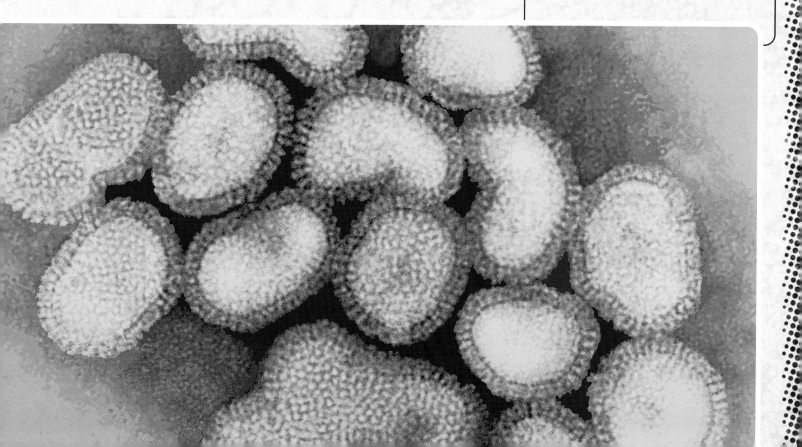

Allergy Alert

On hot summer days, your classroom windows are probably wide open. Some people might begin to sneeze and sniffle, but it is not because they have colds. **Pollen** grains and **spores** in the air are causing hay fever.

Hay fever is an **allergy**—an illness caused when the body overreacts to harmless substances. In hay fever, pollen grains or spores get into the nose and cause it to produce a lot of mucus, as if we have a cold or flu.

These are pollen grains of the hollyhock, Althaea rosea (x850). Pollen grains from different plants can look very different. Many have beautiful shapes.

Pollen causes hay fever sufferers to sneeze.

Pollen

Pollen is not a living thing, but it carries life hidden inside it. It is a very fine, yellow dust produced by flowering plants. Pollen grains are the male sex **cells** of plants, encased in a tough protective coat. If pollen lands on a flower of the same kind of plant, it joins up with egg cells in the flower to make seeds.

Dust from fungi

Pollen is not the only kind of living dust. **Molds** can grow in damp areas of plaster on walls or ceilings. A mold is a kind of **fungus,** and fungi reproduce by releasing clouds of tiny spores. Like pollen, these spores can cause allergies.

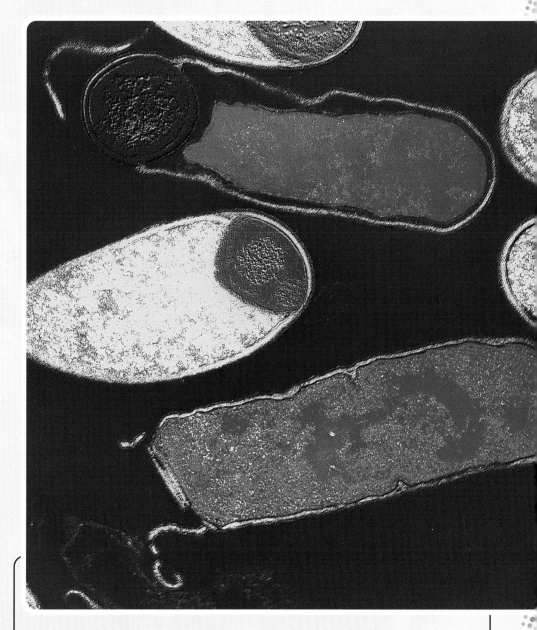

The oval shapes inside some of these bacteria are developing spores.

Bacterial mummies

Some kinds of bacteria can also make spores, but these are not the same as the spores of fungi. A bacterial spore is a sort of sleeping bacterium. There is no food and little moisture in the air. Without protection, most bacteria would quickly die. So a spore-forming bacterium protects its **genes.** It makes a copy of the genes. Then it builds up a series of protective coatings around them. The result is a spore.

Inside their protective spores, the genes can survive drying out, high temperatures, and even radiation. When water and food are available again, the bacterium comes to life.

Chewing Up Old Books

Old textbooks or classwork are sometimes left in storage for months. They make a perfect home for booklice. Booklice are almost microscopic, see-through insects that live in books and papers. Booklice are not true lice, although they are closely related. Booklice are also related to **aphids** and look quite similar to them.

Booklice have chewing mouthparts designed to scrape food from a surface and grind it up.

When a female animal or plant's eggs develop without needing a male to fertilize them, it is called **parthenogenesis.**

Aphids as well as booklice reproduce this way. During the summer months, all aphids that are born are wingless females. These aphids can lay eggs without the need for **fertilization.** But eggs that hatch as fall approaches produce winged male and female aphids. The males and females mate, and the female lays her eggs before the winter comes. The eggs lay in a kind of sleep over winter, then hatch the next spring.

Harmless guests

Booklice are tiny, white, wingless insects that are hard to spot without a flashlight and a magnifying glass. Booklice do not bite or cause disease, so small numbers of them can live in a building completely unnoticed. However, large numbers can cause damage to books, furnishings, and wallpaper.

Booklice eat **cereals, pollen,** pieces of dead insects, and the starchy paste that is used in book binding. But their favorite foods are **mold** and **mildew.** They like warmth and damp, and they avoid bright light. A pile of moldy old books in a warm, damp basement is a booklouse's idea of heaven!

All girls

Booklice are nearly all female. Males are very rare. Booklice eggs develop without being fertilized by a male. Each female lays about 60 eggs. She puts the eggs near a source of food so that when the young **nymphs** hatch, their first meal is all ready for them to eat.

⬆ Aphids, like booklice, are unusual because they can lay eggs and can give birth to live young. Not many animals can do both.

Silverfish and Firebrats

In a damp spot near the sink you might find some other hidden residents. Silverfish are over 0.4 inch (1 cm) long, but you are unlikely to see them. They hide during the day and come out at night to eat.

This is a silverfish on paper. Insects always have three parts to their bodies—the head, the **thorax** (middle), and the **abdomen** (back part). In silverfish each of these body parts is divided into several segments.

Silverfish

Silverfish are flat, long, narrow insects. They get their name from the shiny, silvery-gray scales that cover their bodies. They have two antennae, or feelers, on their head and three long, thin bristles on their tail. Silverfish and their relatives are sometimes called bristletails.

Silverfish live in cool, damp places such as around sinks and bathtubs or in damp basements. Silverfish hide during the day, but at night they come out looking for water and food.

Like booklice, silverfish enjoy book bindings and paste. But they eat a much wider range of food than booklice, including glue, wallpaper paste, photographs, fabrics, **cereals,** and leather.

Many insects live only a few weeks or months, but silverfish can live for three or four years. Female silverfish lay more than 100 eggs during a lifetime. The young that hatch look like small adults, except that they are white rather than silvery-gray.

Both silverfish and firebrats are tough creatures. They can survive for many months without food.

Firebrats

Firebrats look similar to silverfish, except that they are spotty gray rather than silvery. The two are closely related, but firebrats like warm, dry places rather than damp ones. They can live in the school boiler room or in the insulation around central heating pipes.

THE EARLIEST INSECTS?

Many types of insects have lost their wings over time. The ancestors of booklice were winged, but over millions of years they lost their wings because wings were of no use in their **environment.**

But silverfish are different—their ancestors never had wings. They are **primitive** insects, which means that they are like the very earliest types of insects.

Table of Sizes

Although all hidden life is tiny, there is a huge range of sizes. To a flea, a grain of pollen seems just as tiny as the flea seems to us.

These organisms are 20 times bigger than normal.

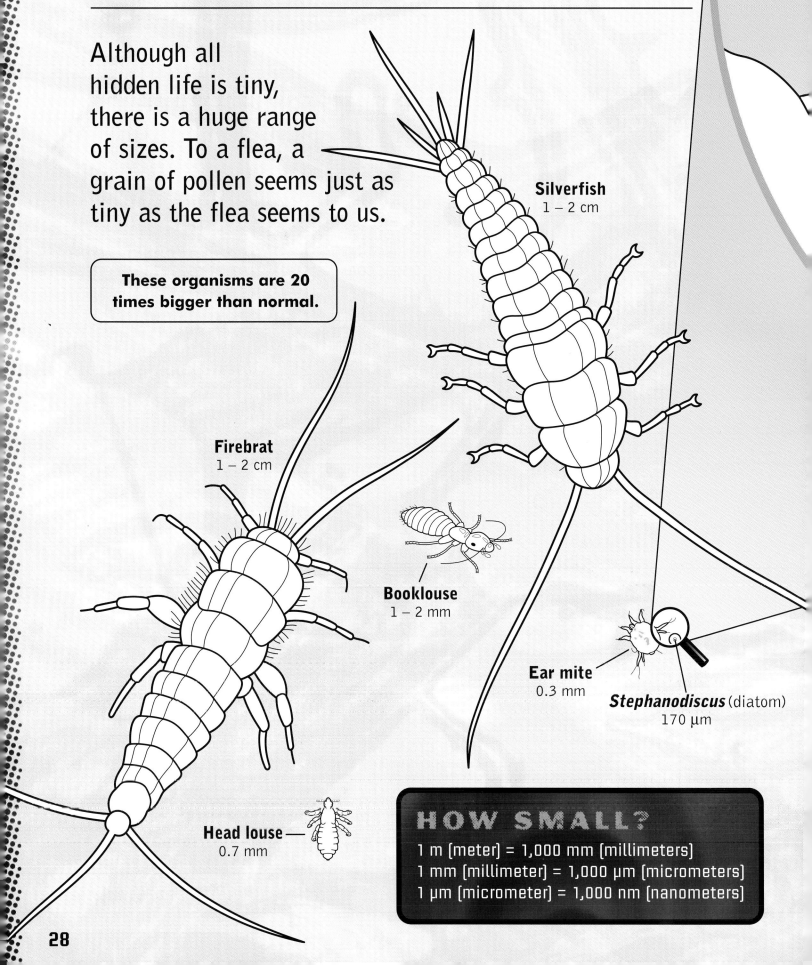

Silverfish
1 – 2 cm

Firebrat
1 – 2 cm

Booklouse
1 – 2 mm

Ear mite
0.3 mm

Stephanodiscus (diatom)
170 µm

Head louse —
0.7 mm

HOW SMALL?

1 m (meter) = 1,000 mm (millimeters)
1 mm (millimeter) = 1,000 µm (micrometers)
1 µm (micrometer) = 1,000 nm (nanometers)

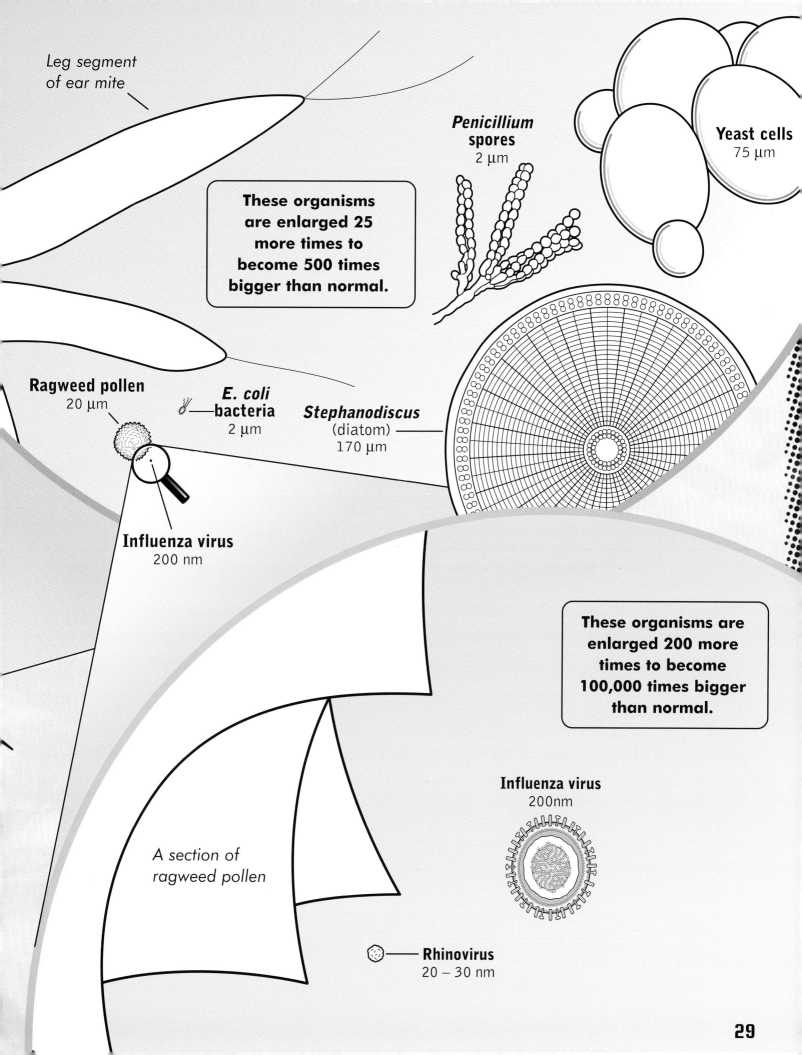

Leg segment
of ear mite

Penicillium
spores
2 μm

Yeast cells
75 μm

These organisms
are enlarged 25
more times to
become 500 times
bigger than normal.

Ragweed pollen
20 μm

E. coli
bacteria
2 μm

Stephanodiscus
(diatom)
170 μm

Influenza virus
200 nm

These organisms are
enlarged 200 more
times to become
100,000 times bigger
than normal.

Influenza virus
200nm

A section of
ragweed pollen

Rhinovirus
20 – 30 nm

29

Glossary

abdomen back section of an insect, which contains most of the body organs

algae members of large group of plantlike creatures, most of which are microscopic

allergy/allergic condition in which the body overreacts to something that is breathed in, eaten, or gets on the skin. It can cause sneezing, rash, or sickness.

antennae the two feelers on an insect's head

aphid small insect that lives on plants and sucks their sap

bacteria microscopic creatures, each one only a single cell. They are different from other single-celled creatures because they do not have a nucleus. Only one of these living things is called a bacterium.

carbon dioxide gas that is found in small amounts in the air

cells building blocks of living things. Some living things are single cells, while others are made up of billions of cells working together.

cereal wheat, barley, oats, and similar food crops

chlorophyll green pigment (colored chemical) found in plants that traps light energy from the sun. The plants use the energy to make food.

chloroplast tiny part within plant cells that turns light energy into food

cyanobacterium type of bacterium that can make their own food from light, water and carbon dioxide, like plants can

deutonymph third stage in the growth of some mites

diatom type of algae found in fresh water or seawater that has a skeleton made of a substance called silica

electron microscope very powerful microscope that can magnify objects up to 500,000 times

environment place where a living thing lives, and the other creatures that live there

ferment to turn sugar in food into another substance, such as an acid or alcohol, by the action of tiny microbes

fertilization when a male sex cell joins with the egg cell of a female to form a new life

fungus plantlike living thing such as a mushroom or a yeast. Two or more of these organisms are called fungi.

genes contain information that enables a cell to build itself, get energy, grow and reproduce

host animal or plant on which a parasite lives

larva the young stage of some types of insects. A larva looks different from an adult and has to go through a changing stage (the pupa) in order to become an adult. More than one larva are larvae.

metabolism all the chemical activity that goes on inside a living cell or collection of cells

microbe microscopic creature such as a bacterium, protozoan, fungus, or virus

microscope instrument for magnifying tiny objects

mildew fungus that infects plants and shows as a powdery covering on affected parts of the plant

mold type of fungus that can grow on or in a wide range of substances, from damp plaster to cheese

molt to shed hair, feathers, or skin

nymph the young of some types of insects and mites. Nymphs usually look similar to their parents and change gradually into adults during several molts.

parasite creature that lives on or in another living creature and takes its food, without giving any benefit in return and sometimes causing harm

parthenogenesis form of reproduction in which eggs develop into young without being fertilized

pollen fine powder produced by flowers to fertilize other flowers

predator animal that hunts and kills another animal for food

primitive being in an ancient or early state. A primitive creature is one that is like its early ancestors.

protein important group of living substances that are used to build structures within living things, and to control the thousands of chemical reactions that happen inside cells

protonymph second stage in the growth of some mites

rennet material made from the stomachs of young calves that is used to curdle milk in cheese making

sensory hair hair on the body of a creature that is sensitive to touch or vibrations

sewage watery wastes from the toilets and drains of houses and from factories

spore very tiny seedlike structure that a fungus uses to reproduce. A bacterial spore is a bacterium that has formed a tough outer coat to help it survive difficult conditions.

thorax middle section of an insect's body that includes the legs, and wings, if it has them

virus very tiny microbe that has to infect a living cell in order to grow or reproduce

xanthan a gummy substance formed by certain types of bacteria

More Books to Read

Burnie, David. *Microlife.* New York: Dorling Kindersley, 1999.

Editorial staff. *Microscopic Investigations: Insects and Spiders.* Vernon Hills, Ill.: Learning Resources, 2001.

Levine, Shar, and Leslie Johnstone. *Science Experiments with a Microscope.* New York: Sterling Publishing, 2003.

Thomas, Ann. *Dairy Products.* Broomall, Penn.: Chelsea House Publishers, 2003.

Snedden Robert. *Microlife: A World of Microorganisms.* Chicago: Heinemann Library, 2000.

An older reader can help you with this book:

Rainis, Kenneth G. *Microscope Science Projects and Experiments: Magnifying the Hidden World.* Berkeley Heights, N.J.: Enslow Publishers, 2003.

Index